Editors
Karen Tam Froloff
Eric Migliaccio

Managing Editor
Ina Massler Levin, M.A.

Editor-in-Chief
Sharon Coan, M.S. Ed.

Cover Artist
Janet Chadwick

Art Manager
Kevin Barnes

Art Director
CJae Froshay

Imaging
Temo Perra
Rosa C. See

Product Manager
Phil Garcia

Publishers
Rachelle Cracchiolo, M.S. Ed.
Mary Dupuy Smith, M.S. Ed.

Author

Melissa Hart, M.F.A.

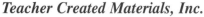

Teacher Created Materials, Inc.
6421 Industry Way
Westminster, CA 92683
www.teachercreated.com
ISBN-0-7439-3781-3
©2003 Teacher Created Materials, Inc.
Made in U.S.A.

Table of Contents

Introduction. 3

Complete Sentences 4

Nouns 5

Possessive Nouns 6

Irregular Plural Nouns 7

Pronouns 8

Pronoun Agreement 9

Verbs 10

Irregular Verbs 11

Subject and Verb Agreement 12

Sentence Fragments 13

Adjectives 14

Adverbs. 16

Prepositions. 18

Putting It All Together I 20

Coordinating Conjunctions. 21

Run-on Sentences 22

Exclamatory Sentences. 23

Capitalization 24

Periods. 26

Commas 27

Putting It All Together II. 28

Apostrophes in Contractions and Possessives 29

Quotation Marks. 31

Colons 33

Semicolons 34

Hyphens and Dashes. 35

Putting It All Together III 36

Short Story 37

Assessment 39

Answer Key 45

Introduction

The idea that "practice makes perfect" relates directly to your child's education. The more practice your child receives in concepts being taught in school, the more success he or she will achieve. Many parents know the value of practicing a subject learned in school, but the lack of readily available resources can be frustrating.

As a parent, it is also difficult to know where to focus your efforts so that the practice your child receives at home supports what is being taught at school.

This book was written with the goal of helping both parents and teachers to reinforce basic language skills with children. *Practice Makes Perfect: Grammar, Usage & Mechanics* reviews grammar skills for sixth grade students. The exercises in this book can be completed sequentially or out of order, as needed.

Completing this book will help your child meet the following sixth grade standards and objectives, similar to those required by your state and school district:

- The student uses simple and compound sentences in written compositions.
- The student uses pronouns, nouns, verbs, adjectives, adverbs, prepositions, and coordinating conjunctions in written compositions.
- The student uses conventions of capitalization and punctuation in written compositions.
- The student uses strategies to organize written work.
- The student evaluates own and others' writing.
- The student uses strategies to draft and revise written work.

How to Make the Most of This Book

Here are some ideas to think about when using this book:

- Set aside a special place in your home for grammar practice. Keep the area neat, with the book and favorite writing implements close at hand.
- Set up a particular time of day to work on practice pages. This establishes consistency.
- Make sure your child understands the written instructions at the top of each practice page.
- Keep all practice sessions with your child positive. If your child becomes frustrated, set the book aside for a period of time and come back to it later.
- Review the work your child has done.
- Pay attention to those areas in which your child has the most difficulty. Provide extra guidance and further practice in those areas.

Complete Sentences

A **complete sentence** contains a subject and a predicate.

- The subject tells who or what the sentence is about.

    Examples: (Jim Henson) created a group of puppets he called Muppets.

    (An old, green coat) became the material for the first Kermit the Frog.

- The predicate tells what the subject is or does. The verb is found in the predicate.

    Example: *The Muppet Show* <u>entertained</u> both children and adults for years.

    Miss Piggy *is* <u>Kermit the Frog's eager girlfriend.</u>

Look at the sentences below. Circle the subject, and underline the predicate.

1. (Great-horned owls) <u>are at the top of the food chain.</u>

2. (They) <u>can survive almost anywhere.</u>

3. (These owls) <u>eat rodents, insects, and even skunks.</u>

4. (Outdoor cats) <u>are not safe from these winged predators.</u>

5. (The ears on Great-horned owls) <u>are lopsided.</u>

6. This <u>allows</u> (them) to pinpoint the exact location of their prey.

7. (A Great-horned owl's eyes) <u>work like binoculars.</u>

8. (No small animal, bird, or insect) <u>can hide from these owls.</u>

9. (The flight feathers on a Great-horned owl) <u>are serrated.</u>

10. (These feathers) <u>allow the owl to fly silently through the forest.</u>

11. (Cliffs and trees) <u>make excellent nesting sites for owls.</u>

12. (Other birds' nests) <u>are fair game, too.</u>

13. (Great-horned owls) <u>are amazing creatures.</u>

14. (You) <u>can see them at dusk.</u>

15. (Their call) <u>is distinctive and haunting.</u>

Nouns

There are two types of **nouns**—common and proper.

- **Common nouns** describe any one person, place, or thing.

  Examples: That young *man* works at two different jobs after school.

  The toy *store* is a fun and exciting place to work.

- **Proper nouns** describe a specific person, place, or thing and are capitalized.

  Examples: *New York City* offers thousands of job opportunities.

  John Smith can't wait to move there.

Part I: Change the underlined common nouns below into proper nouns and the underlined proper nouns into common nouns. Then rewrite the sentence in the space provided.

1. I've always wanted to see <u>Italy</u>. _____
2. <u>Kathy Petrini</u> owns the <u>restaurant</u> downtown. *A girl I know owns Little Italy downtown.*
3. <u>Mr. Minelli</u> drives a red <u>Honda</u>. *Our neighbor drives a red car.*
4. <u>George</u> likes to play <u>badminton</u>. *My friend likes to play Competitive Badminton.*
5. <u>Main Street Deli</u> offers free <u>cookies</u> on Fridays. *The deli offers free Chips Ahoy on Friday*
6. <u>My brother</u> watches <u>Bugs Bunny</u> on Saturday mornings. *Levi watches cartoons on Saturday mornings.*

Here are two sub-types of nouns: compound and collective.

- **Compound nouns** are two or more nouns that function as a single unit.

  Examples: The <u>commander-in-chief</u> fought in World War II.

- **Collective nouns** name groups of people or things.

  A *crowd* of people poured into the baseball stadium.

Part II: Underline the compound or collective nouns in the sentences below.

1. A happy family went to the beach one sunny Saturday.
2. My sister-in-law is knitting me a sweater for Christmas.
3. We rode the trolley car all the way downtown.
4. Jackson led the herd of cattle into the stable.
5. Our class toured the Smithsonian on a field trip.
6. Did you know that the editor-in-chief of the magazine worked in the circus?
7. Rake up that pile of leaves, please.
8. We asked the passers-by if they wanted their cars washed.
9. A flock of Canadian geese flew overhead.
10. The group of carolers sang beautifully.

Possessive Nouns

Possessive nouns show ownership. To show possession with a singular noun, add an *apostrophe* and an *s*.

      Examples: girl's science book, student's locker

With plural nouns ending in *s*, add an *apostrophe* after the *s*.

      Examples: *boys'* homework, *teachers'* lounge

When a plural noun does not end in *s*, add an *apostrophe* and an *s*.

      Examples: *mice's cages, women's* shoes

Study the sentences below. Then rewrite the sentences correctly, changing possessive nouns as needed.

1. Pauls' bicycle has thick tires and a sturdy frame.
   _____ *Paul's* _____

2. He uses it to ride up his citys' steep hills.
   _____ *city's* _____

3. The other boys bicycles aren't quite as sturdy.
   _____ *boys'* _____

4. Paul often rides alone, near the days end.
   _____ *days'* _____

5. Once, a womens' bicycling team passed him on a hill.
   _____ *AI* _____

6. The boys' pride was stung, and he was determined to ride faster.
   _____ *boy's* _____

7. He trained until his muscles bulged.
   _____ *muscles'* _____

8. He pumped up his bikes' tires and got ready to go.
   _____ *AI* _____

9. Paul started out on the months chilliest morning.
   _____ *months'* _____

10. Halfway up the mountain, a thorns' sharp edges pricked his tire.
    _____ *AI* _____

11. Paul changed his tire, using his fathers tools.
    _____ *fathers'* _____

12. Geese stared at the boy.
    _____ *AI* _____

13. Paul could hear the geeses' honking for miles around.
    _____ *geese's* _____

14. He rode hard, to his hearts delight.
    _____ *heart's* _____

15. Swiftly, a girls scouting troop passed him on a hill.
    _____ *girl's* _____

Irregular Plural Nouns

A **plural noun** indicates more than one person, place, or thing. To form the plural of regular nouns, simply add an *s*, such as in *bears* and *lawyers*.

Here are some rules for forming irregular plural nouns.

- To form the plural of nouns ending in *s, sh, ch,* or *x*, add *es*.

    Examples: All of the fifth-grade classes went home early. (class → classes)

    We moved those heavy *boxes* upstairs. (box → boxes)

- If a noun ends in the consonant *y*, change the *y* to *i* and add *es*.

    Examples: They hope to travel to four *cities* in Europe. (city → cities)

    Those *ladies* collected food for hungry children. (lady → ladies)

- Finally, if the noun ends with *vowel + y*, add an *s*.

    Examples: There was a crowd around the *monkeys* at the zoo. (monkey → monkeys)

Part I: Write the irregular plural form beside the singular nouns below.

1. baby _____
2. match _____
3. fox _____
4. turkey _____
5. party _____
6. dress _____
7. lily _____

8. cry _____
9. fish _____
10. city _____
11. crutch _____
12. key _____
13. hex _____
14. lunch _____

Here are some more rules for making singular nouns plural.

- Add an *s* to most nouns ending in *f*.

    Examples: The *chiefs* met for a conference. (chief → chiefs)

- In some cases, change the *f* or *fe* to *v* and add *s*.

    Examples: *Wolves* have migrated back to Oregon recently. (wolf → wolves)

- In most compound words, make the main word plural.

    Examples: The *fathers-in-law* sat on the right side of the church.

- Some nouns change their spelling when they become plural.

    Examples: *child* to *children*, *goose* to *geese*, *man* to *men*, *tooth* to *teeth*

- And some nouns have the same form whether they are singular or plural.

    Examples: *swine, deer, series, sheep, species*

Write the plural form beside the singular nouns below.

1. belief _____
2. goose _____
3. sister-in-law _____
4. wolf _____
5. man _____

6. sheep _____
7. passerby _____
8. foot _____
9. deer _____
10. chief _____

Pronouns

A **pronoun** is a word used in the place of a noun or another pronoun.

Examples: First person (I, me, my, we, us, our, ours)
Second person (you, your, yours)
Third person (he, him, his, she, her, hers, it, its, they, them, their, theirs)

Good writers use pronouns to avoid tedious repetition in their writing.

Here is an example of a repetitious sentence:

Mrs. Catchatori gave Mrs. Catchatori's car to Mrs. Catchatori's husband, Mr. Catchatori. Mr. Catchatori loved the car.

Here is the same sentence which has been revised using pronouns:

Mrs. Catchatori gave her car to her husband. He loved it.

Read the story below. Cross out repetitious nouns when needed, and rewrite the story with appropriate pronouns.

Sixth Grade Nature Camp

Connie looked forward to Sixth Grade Nature Camp with all Connie's heart. Her friends Joanne, Debi, and Lyddie could hardly wait, either. On the morning Connie, Joanne, Debi, and Lyddie were to go to camp, Connie, Joanne, Debi, and Lyddie put Connie, Joanne, Debi, and Lyddie's suitcases in the bus. Connie sat down next to Connie's best friend. The driver started the bus and guided the bus out onto the road. The bus climbed high into the mountains. The mountains were beautiful, with trees thickly covering the mountains. Connie and Connie's friend stared out the window in delight. "Connie is so happy she finally gets to go to camp!" Connie told Connie's friend. The boy behind her took a picture of Connie with the boy's camera. "Smile!" the boy said to Connie, and Connie smiled Connie's best smile. The driver pulled the bus into a parking lot, and the driver helped the kids get their bags off the bus. It was time to camp!

Pronoun Agreement

Pronouns must agree with their **antecedents** (the words to which they refer).

Example: **Cathy** will borrow a flashlight, which **she** needs to go spelunking.
    (antecedent)   (pronoun)

Pronouns must match their antecedents in number, person, and gender.

Examples: **My fish and my turtle** both love **their** snack of mealworms. (*number*)

If **anyone** wants cake, **he** or **she** had better come to the cafeteria now. (person)

Martin gave his calculator to his mother. (*gender*)

Part I: In the sentences below, fill in the correct pronoun to agree with the underlined antecedent.

1. Each student should wear _____ gown and graduation cap.

2. Mari wants to give _____ old records to her grandmother.

3. We want to take _____ vacation in May.

4. Each person needs to put on _____ coat and get ready!

5. Mom and her sisters shared _____ picnic lunch with a homeless man.

6. Jimmy and _____ dog love to hike in the mountains.

7. Mara and Cindy brush _____ hair a hundred times a night.

8. Every teacher must wear _____ best clothes to the conference.

9. Robert carried _____ backpack in one hand.

10. The monkeys swung eagerly in _____ cage.

Part II: Now, use the pronouns below to create 10 sentences, making sure to use the correct antecedent.

1. his or her _____

2. their _____

3. his _____

4. she _____

5. his or her _____

6. they _____

7. he _____

8. my _____

9. its _____

10. our _____

Verbs

Verbs are words that name an action or describe a state of being. There are three basic types of verbs:

- **Action verbs** tell what a subject does. They often show some kind of action.
  Examples: Molly *laughed* at the comedian.
  The truck *rolled* downhill.

- **Linking verbs** help the words at the end of a sentence describe the subject.
  Examples: Aunt Suzie *is* my mother's cousin.
  The clown *was* happy all the time.

- **Helping verbs** are added to another verb to make the meaning clearer.
  Examples: They *will* run at lunchtime.
  She *could* play the piano tonight.

Part I: Study the sentences below. In the space beside the sentence, write the appropriate type of verb (**action**, **linking**, or **helping**) that is being used.

1. Cathy and Taylor were exhausted from studying. _____
2. He was swimming in the Pacific ocean. _____
3. The dog attacked the raccoon in the forest. _____
4. My mother will crochet a blanket for my sister's birthday. _____
5. That teacher yells a lot. _____
6. We are excited about the party next weekend. _____
7. I have purchased a beautiful snowboard. _____
8. That model plane flies really well. _____
9. Martha is happy that her play will be produced. _____
10. The rattlesnake will not bite unless you provoke it. _____

Part II: Now, write sentences of your own, using the type of verb listed.

1. action verb _____

    _____

2. linking verb _____

    _____

3. helping verb _____

    _____

4. action verb _____

    _____

5. linking verb _____

    _____

6. helping verb _____

    _____

Irregular Verbs

Many verbs end in *ed* when you put them into the past tense.

    Examples: The driver *honked* the horn.

               We *walked* six miles to the park.

For some verbs, you do not simply add an *ed* to put them into past tense. They are called irregular verbs.

    Examples:

Present tense	Past tense
spy	spied
hide	hid
bring	brought

Part I: Write the following irregular verbs in the past tense.

1. fly _____
2. swim _____
3. cry _____
4. drink _____
5. go _____
6. speed _____
7. run _____
8. sing _____
9. draw _____
10. eat _____

11. buy _____
12. speak _____
13. ride _____
14. wear _____
15. grow _____
16. freeze _____
17. make _____
18. sleep _____
19. bite _____
20. send _____

Sometimes, other words in the sentence can give clues as to which tense the verb should be in. Words such as *yesterday, last month,* and *previously* show that the action occurred in the past. Words such as *tomorrow, in the future,* and *next week* show that the action will occur in the future. Likewise, verbs in the same sentence often share the same tense.

Part II: Add a verb to each of the sentences below. Choose from the words in parentheses. Make sure your choice is in the appropriate tense.

1. Last week, we _____ to the opera.

2. Today, I _____ exhausted, and I can't stop yawning.

3. In 2000, my family _____ a huge party.

4. Shirley _____ when I say, "You know?"

5. We ran quickly; our friend _____ very slowly.

6. Jesse James _____ in her farmhouse in the late 1800s.

7. Tomorrow, we _____ to the movies.

8. Yesterday, I _____ the school's record for long jump.

9. In the year 3000, people _____ on Mars.

10. Yesterday, I _____ twenty dollars.

Subject and Verb Agreement

Subjects may be singular or plural. The verb form must agree with the subject.

Examples: We was calling out the cat's name. (incorrect)
We were calling out the cat's name. (correct)

Use the following steps to make sure your verb agrees with your subject:

1. Find the subject of the sentence.

2. Decide whether the subject is singular or plural.

3. Select the appropriate verb form to match the subject.

Study the story below. Cross out inappropriate verb forms and rewrite the story in the space below, using the correct verb forms.

Seven students is planning a trip to the snow. We is going to ski, snowshoe, and sled until we is so tired that we falls into bed at night. My mom will go, and she are really excited about making hot chocolate for all of us. She just boughts new skis for the occasion. I needs new long underwear, and I could uses a hat and some mittens. My friend Joe want a snowboard; his mom are going to buy him one for his birthday. My friends and I is looking for cabins to rent. We is having a car wash to raise money. I hopes to get good at skiing so I can joins my friends on the intermediate slopes. Winter sports is a lot of fun, as long as you has the right equipment and warm clothes.

_____

_____

_____

_____

_____

_____

_____

_____

_____

_____

_____

_____

Sentence Fragments

Sentence fragments occur when a sentence is missing either a subject or a verb. (They are also called incomplete sentences.)

Examples: **Incorrect**—going to the circus tomorrow.

Problem—Who is going to the circus? The sentence is missing a subject.
Correction—Judy and Flanders are going to the circus tomorrow.
Incorrect—My two cats, Iago and Alger.
Problem—What action is occurring? The sentence is missing a verb.
Correction—My two cats, Iago and Alger, love to sleep in the laundry basket together.

Part I: Study the sentences below. Decide whether each sentence is missing a subject or a verb. Write "subject" or "verb" in the space beside each sentence.

1. watching the hockey game_____

2. is an excellent actress_____

3. can juggle six apples _____

4. were looking for the lost dog_____

5. the old, battered suitcase _____

6. Los Angeles, California _____

7. the red convertible _____

8. is studying earthquakes _____

9. won't make it to your party _____

10. Mother's antique dishes _____

Part II: Now, rewrite each fragment, adding either a subject or a verb to make a complete sentence.

1. _____

2. _____

3. _____

4. _____

5. _____

6. _____

7. _____

8. _____

9. _____

10. _____

Adjectives

Adjectives are words that describe either nouns or pronouns. They answer these questions: What kind? How many? Which one? How much?

Examples: She wore a ring in her nose. (*What kind?*)

She wore a *silver* ring in her nose.

We served dinner to people. (*How many?*)

We served dinner to *forty* people.

Thomas gave a dollar to the man on the corner. (*Which one?*)

Thomas gave a dollar to the *homeless man* on the corner.

I need to buy sugar. (*How much?*)

I need to buy *three boxes* of sugar.

Part I: Rewrite the following sentences, adding adjectives to answer the questions.

1. Georgina likes her dance class. (*What kind?*)

   _____

2. People crowded into the stadium for the concert. (*How many?*)

   _____

3. I won the stuffed bear. (*Which one?*)

   _____

4. Mickey earned quarters for doing chores. (*How much?*)

   _____

There are three types of adjectives:

- **Common adjectives** describe nouns or pronouns
  Example: The *strong* woman lifted boxes into the truck.

- **Proper adjectives** are formed from proper nouns.
  Example: She studied *Egyptian* art in college.

- **Compound adjectives** are made up of more than one word. They are sometimes hyphenated.
  Examples: My brother is in his *teenage* years. He is living in a *far-off* place.

Part II: Add adjectives to the sentences below, according to the type listed after each sentence.

1. My _____ brother hates avocados and tomatoes. (*common adjective*)
2. Pizza and lasagna are Jake's favorite _____ food. (*proper adjective*)
3. _____ smoking is a serious problem in high schools. (*compound adjective*)
4. Every summer, we go to the _____ Ocean. (*proper adjective*)
5. Her _____ dress cost twenty dollars. (*common adjective*)
6. Janice's _____ daughter will be driving soon. (*compound adjective*)
7. The explorers hiked to the _____ Pole. (*proper adjective*)
8. She drives a _____ truck. (*common adjective*)
9. There's a grocery store _____ my house. (*compound adjective*)
10. "That was a _____ movie!" cried Kathryn. (*common adjective*)

Adjectives *(cont.)*

Write a one-page story using all of the adjectives in the box below.

Egyptian	spotted	white	shocked
crunchy	tasty	lazy	invisible
huge	rough	jagged	unknown
nervous	poor	noisy	dark

_____

_____

_____

_____

_____

_____

_____

_____

_____

_____

_____

_____

_____

_____

_____

_____

_____

_____

_____

Adverbs

Adverbs are words that describe verbs, adjectives, or other adverbs. They answer these questions: When? To what extent? How?

Examples: My father ran. (*When?*)
My father ran *yesterday*.
Maribelle sang. (*How?*)
Maribelle sang *badly*.
She finished her homework. (To what *extent?*)
She *partially* finished her homework.

Most adverbs are formed by adding *ly* to an adjective. Here are some examples:

Adjective	Adverb
soft	softly
sad	sadly
beautiful	beautifully
quick	quickly
mad	madly

Other adverbs do not end in *ly*. Here are some examples:

• already   • often   • far   • now   • more   • soon

Part I: Rewrite the following sentences, adding adverbs to answer the questions below.

1. The monkey did tricks for the crowd. (*When?*)

   _____

2. The teacher gave the instructions. (*How?*)

   _____

3. I ate my dinner. (*To what extent?*)

   _____

Part II: Add adverbs to the sentences below to correspond with the question after each sentence.

1. I _____ understand your argument. (*To what extent?*)

2. We're moving _____ to a new city. (*When?*)

3. My older brother sings _____ in the shower. (*How?*)

4. The tree fell _____. (*How?*)

Adverbs *(cont.)*

Write a one-page story using all of the adverbs in the box below.

eagerly	ridiculously	almost	joyously
sadly	afterward	skeptically	occasionally
delicately	splendidly	anxiously	shockingly
tomorrow	quietly	never	quickly

_____

_____

_____

_____

_____

_____

_____

_____

_____

_____

_____

_____

_____

_____

_____

_____

_____

_____

_____

_____

Prepositions

Prepositions are words that link a noun or pronoun to another word in the sentence. Here is a list of some of the most common prepositions:

above	between	outside	beneath	over
behind	during	around	on	into
across	in	at	from	through
after	inside	under	out	up

Part I: Circle the prepositions in the following sentences.

1. My grandparents performed in the circus.

2. Grandpa used to walk on the tightwire.

3. Beneath him, the audience gasped.

4. Grandma stood on the back of a horse.

5. It galloped around the ring, but she never fell.

6. During the performance, people sold popcorn.

7. Kids crowded across benches, talking and laughing.

8. Between acts, my grandparents mended costumes.

9. They helped feed the elephants for a few extra dollars.

10. With that money, they saved for a trailer.

11. They lived inside that trailer for a long time.

12. They ate most of their meals outside.

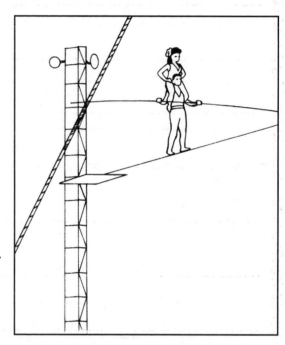

Part II: Now, add prepositions to complete the following sentences.

1. The treasure is buried _____ a bridge.

2. First, you have to walk ten paces _____ a field.

3. Then you have to crawl _____ a barbed wire fence.

4. Later, you'll see a white dot _____ a tree.

5. Turn right, and walk _____ a hill.

6. Watch out _____ you because there is a stray dog.

7. _____ this point, you'll see a crooked tree.

8. Climb _____ it and look to your left.

9. You'll see the bridge _____ the tree.

10. Dig a hole _____ the big green boulder.

11. You'll see a box _____ a few minutes.

12. There, _____ the box, is the treasure!

Prepositions *(cont.)*

Describe how to play your favorite sport or game. Use at least 15 prepositions. After you're finished with your description, circle the prepositions. How many did you use?

_____

_____

_____

_____

_____

_____

_____

_____

_____

_____

_____

_____

Putting It All Together I

Use the following words to create 15 sentences. You can change the forms of the words (tense, singular to plural) as needed. Try to use one word from each list in each sentence. Try not to use any word twice.

Nouns	Verbs	Adjectives	Adverbs	Prepositions
scientist	shout	sad	quietly	into
squirrel	sniff	chilly	energetically	before
football	giggle	complicated	dismally	until
palm tree	consider	green	respectfully	over
asphalt	ski	enormous	yesterday	in
George	fly	miniscule	loudly	beneath
kangaroo	pedal	sweet	happily	through
macaroni	stare	confused	urgently	around
girl	shriek	awkward	seriously	below
ice cube	dance	sleepy	encouragingly	inside
broccoli	try	pink	messily	during
sunflower	jump	fast	softly	under
Agnes	roar	silent	despondently	on
cat	glare	filthy	sloppily	outside
bicycle	hop	sticky	weirdly	over
				above

1. _____
2. _____
3. _____
4. _____
5. _____
6. _____
7. _____
8. _____
9. _____
10. _____
11. _____
12. _____
13. _____
14. _____
15. _____

Coordinating Conjunctions

A **coordinating conjunction** links two sentences together. A comma comes before a coordinating conjunction.

Examples: I like hard rock music, <u>but</u> my father doesn't want me to play it.

Jerry is poor, <u>so</u> he can't buy tickets to the opera.

Here are the seven coordinating conjunctions:

• for   • and   • nor   • but   • or   • yet   • so

You can see that lined up in this manner, they form the *mnemonic* (a memory tool) called "fanboys." A mnemonic uses the first letter of each word to form a word or sentence that is easy to remember.

Part I: Study the following sentences. Circle the subject, underline the predicate, and draw a box around the coordinating conjunction.

1. He didn't bring the soup, nor did he remember bread.

2. I trained for months, yet I couldn't finish the race.

3. Would you like to ski, or would you prefer to snowboard?

4. I don't know Spanish, but I do know some French.

5. She saw the movie three times, for she really loved the leading actress.

6. The postal worker is here, so I have to answer the door.

7. They raise Angora cats, and they also have three dogs.

Part II: Now, study the pairs of sentences below. Using coordinating conjunctions, rewrite each pair of sentences to make one sentence. Don't forget the comma.

1. The shoes did not fit. The dress fit perfectly. _____

   _____

2. Jackson's dog ran down the street. It stopped at the crosswalk. _____

   _____

3. I'm excited. It's my birthday today. _____

   _____

4. New York is a beautiful state. It gets quite cold. _____

   _____

5. Mother loves the opera. She used to sing in college. _____

   _____

6. That nursery sells Christmas trees. It is February. _____

   _____

7. Marcus rode the unicycle. He has excellent balance. _____

   _____

8. Mary's cats sit on the couch. She doesn't allow them on the table. _____

   _____

Run-on Sentences

Run-on sentences occur in one of two ways.

☞ In the first type of run-on, the sentence is missing punctuation and/or a coordinating conjunction.

Examples: She went to Australia she saw a kangaroo. (*run-on*)

She went to Australia. She saw a kangaroo. (*correct*)

She went to Australia, and she saw a kangaroo. (*correct*)

Part I: Study the run-on sentences below. Fix them by adding a period or a comma and a coordinating conjunction.

1. Molly bought groceries she also bought flowers.

2. Tracy swims every day she also jogs three miles.

3. Mr. DiMarco drove a red bus he painted it himself.

4. The baby cried it missed its mother.

5. It's Tuesday the cafeteria will be serving pizza.

6. She's chilly she forgot her gloves and a hat.

7. The singer canceled her concert her throat was hurting.

8. You need to take vitamins they keep you healthy.

9. My dog loves the forest he runs all over, sniffing trees.

10. The girl painted a picture she hoped to give it to her mother.

☞ In the second type of run-on sentence, the sentence is missing a word or words.

Examples: We love the baseball team, we see a game every Saturday. (*run-on*)

We love the baseball team, and we see a game every Saturday. (*correct*)

We love the baseball team, so we see a game every Saturday. (*correct*)

Part II: Study the run-on sentences below. Fix them by adding a word or words.

1. She loves hot chocolate, she drinks three cups a day.

2. The soccer game lost the match, they'd practiced for weeks.

3. The doctor is busy, it is flu season.

4. A bird made a nest in his chimney, he had to call a chimney sweep.

5. Grandpa taught me to fish, we caught three trout.

6. Honeybees have a hive in that tree, don't get stung.

7. She loves to take the bus, the passengers are so interesting.

8. Read those three books, take the test on Friday.

9. The photographer gave me the photos, they were extraordinary.

10. Mavis signed copies of her book at the festival, many people wanted to meet her.

Exclamatory Sentences

Exclamatory sentences show strong emotions. They end with an exclamation point.

> Examples: Watch out for that falling tree!
> There's a spider in your shoe!

Study the situations below. Write exclamatory sentences to describe each one. Don't forget an exclamation mark! The first one has been done for you.

1. You open a box on your birthday, and out jumps a puppy.

   Oh, Boy, just what I always wanted!

2. Your father emerges from his office wearing a clown costume.

3. Your little brother throws your favorite CD out the car window.

4. You and your friend are walking down the street, when you spot the ice cream truck.

5. You put on your socks and find that your dog has chewed a hole in both heels.

6. You're trying to sleep, when the telephone rings in your ear.

7. You reach for a frying pan and burn your wrist on the hot stove.

8. You run to kick the soccer ball, slip, and end up flat on your face in the mud.

9. You open your front door, and all your friends yell out, "Surprise! Happy Birthday!"

10. You call your favorite radio station and win tickets to see a band you love.

11. Your baby sister spills stewed prunes all over your book report.

12. You're doing some construction work, when you step on a nail.

13. You're watching a scary movie in the dark, when suddenly something licks your hand.

14. You're jumping curbs on your bicycle, when suddenly the front tire comes off.

15. You're at the park, when a pigeon lands on your head.

Capitalization

Capital letters are used in all sorts of ways. Here are the basic rules. Capitalize the following:

- Titles of people (*Mr., Mrs., Dr.*)
- Names of towns, counties, countries, and states (*Pacific Northwest, Indonesia, San Diego, Arizona*)
- Days of the week and months of the year (*Sunday, February*)
- Street names (*Moss Hollow Road, Deer Creek Lane*)
- Holidays (*Valentine Day, Easter, Christmas*)
- The first word of direct quotations; the first word in a sentence (*Nathan cried, "You have four cats?"*)
- The salutation and closing of a letter (*Dear Sandy; Sincerely, Cassie*)

Study the sentences below. Rewrite each of them, crossing out lowercase letters and replacing them with capital letters, as needed.

1. my friend mike loves to collect old books.

2. Every friday, he goes to mr. beedle's bookstore to look for books.

3. sometimes, mr. Beedle leaves a note for mike on thursday.

4. "dear Mike," it says, "i have a new book for you."

5. "Don't forget to bring your money. sincerely, mr. beedle."

6. The bookstore is located at 323 charnelton lane in philadelphia.

7. mike takes the bus and gets off on franklin street.

8. He walks into the bookstore and says, "hello!"

9. "greetings!" says Mr. beedle. "welcome!"

10. On new year's day, mike invites mr. beedle to his house.

11. "bring your mom!" Mike says.

12. "can I bring dad, too?" Mr. Beedle asks mike.

13. "does he like books?" mike asks.

14. the family shows up at 55 clark street on December 31st.

15. "we brought you socks! mr. beedle's father says to mike.

Capitalization *(cont.)*

Here is a list of other items that are always capitalized:

- Book titles, which are always italicized
- Titles of poems, stories, and songs, which are in quotations
- Magazine and newspaper titles, which are always italicized
- Works of painting, sculpture, etc., which are always italicized
- Nationalities
- Religions
- Schools and school subjects
- Companies and departments of government
- Brand names of products

Study the list below. Cross out lowercase letters and rewrite the words with capitals where needed. Then use all of the words in a short story.

1. cabrillo elementary school

   _____

2. catholic _____

3. cucumbers _____

4. los angeles times _____

5. unicycle _____

6. "frosty the snowman"

   _____

7 charlotte's web _____

8. coca cola _____

9. kitten _____

10. english class _____

11. sony _____

12. italian _____

13. pine tree _____

14. the mona lisa _____

15. university of southern california

    _____

16. toys r us _____

_____

_____

_____

_____

_____

_____

Periods

Use a **period** at the end of a sentence to show where the sentence stops. Periods are also used in initials, abbreviations, and titles before names. If the abbreviation appears at the end of the sentence, you should not add an extra period.

Examples: Someone carved *J.J.* into the oak tree.
Mr. Stevens is the mayor of that town.
I live in the *U.S.A.*

Part I: Study the sentences below. Add periods where needed.

1. JoJo found a suitcase bearing the initials LS.

2. The suitcase sat at the intersection between Main St and Third Ave, under a tree.

3. "Is this yours?" she asked Dr Smith.

4. "No," he said. "Try the Rev Sanders at the Baptist Church."

5. "Is that the church on Blanket St?" asked JoJo.

6. "Yes. Ms Rimbaud should be there now," Dr Smith said.

7. JoJo made a quick stop at her PO box for her mail.

8. Then she took the suitcase to Ms Rimbaud in the church office.

9. "There was no id on this suitcase," she said.

10. Rev Sanders is out buying groceries, paper plates, etc for the church picnic," Ms Rimbaud said.

11. "Leave the suitcase here, and Mr Roberts, the janitor, will give it to him."

12. JoJo drove down Sullivan Rd toward her house.

13. She saw many cars with US flags on their windows.

14. On Lansing Blvd, she pulled into a driveway.

15. There on her doorstep, sat another suitcase bearing the initials JJ.

Part II: Abbreviate the following words, making sure to add periods where needed.

1. Avenue _____

2. Street _____

3. Road _____

4. Place _____

5. Mister _____

6. Missus _____

7. Doctor _____

8. etcetera _____

9. identification _____

10. Post Office _____

11. Reverend _____

12. Boulevard _____

13. United States _____

14. United Parcel Service _____

Commas

You've studied how to use commas with coordinating conjunctions to create a long sentence. Commas are also used in the following ways:

- Use a comma when writing out a date.
  Example: The Declaration of Independence was signed on July 4, 1776.

- Use a comma to separate the names of geographical locations.
  Example: We love the rain in Seattle, Washington.

- Use a comma after greetings and closings in a letter.
  Example: Dear Father, Thank you for my allowance. Love, Pat

Study the sentences below. Add commas where needed.

1. Ms. King teaches sixth graders in Oxnard California.

2. She'll take them to Europe on June 20 2003.

3. First, they'll go to London England.

4. After they see Buckingham Palace, they'll go to Paris France.

5. On July 4th 2003, they'll go to Greece.

6. Athens Greece is the home of the Acropolis.

7. The students will see the birthplace of the Olympics in Olympia Greece.

8. Finally, they'll head for home on July 6th 2003.

9. Their plane stops for an hour in Frankfurt Germany.

10. It lands a day later in Los Angeles California.

11. "Dear Mrs. King" the students wrote.

12. "Thank you for taking us to Europe. Love your students."

13. Mrs. King replied from her home in Oak View California.

14. "Dear students" she typed on her computer.

15. "I had a wonderful time. Did you? Sincerely, Mrs. King."

Putting It All Together II

Study the following sentences and rewrite them on the lines below. Correct punctuation and capitalization, as needed.

1. Mrs mandy murphy checked her PO box this afternoon.

_____

2. There was a invitation from dr Frank simpson

_____

3. "Dear Julie" the letter read.

_____

4. "Please come to a surprise party for Mrs cathy Simpson"

_____

5. "There will be food, beverages, etc, plus a live band"

_____

6. "I hope you can make it. Sincerely Frank."

_____

7. mrs murphy looked at the initials on the bottom of the letter, which read "fs."

_____

8. "Who are the simpsons?" she wondered

_____

9. A woman beside her opened her PO box. "Where is my party invitation" she exclaimed

_____

10. mrs Murphy held out dr. simpon's invitation

_____

11. "is this yours" she asked

_____

12. Ms julie Sheridan looked at the invitation.

_____

13. "yes" she cried "I thought I wasn't invited."

_____

14. "Thank you" she told mrs Murphy. "would you like to come to a surprise party?"

_____

Apostrophes in Contractions and Possessives

Contractions refer to two words, which have been combined. Add an **apostrophe** in the space where a letter or letters have been omitted.

Examples: can + not = can't

you + are = you're

Part I: Study the words below. Write the contraction beside each, making sure to add an apostrophe. Then write the letters that were omitted during the contraction. The first one has been done for you.

1. I + will = _____ *I'll* _____ _____ *wi* _____
2. should + not = _____ _____
3. we + are = _____ _____
4. she + is = _____ _____
5. they + are = _____ _____
6. I + am = _____ _____
7. could + not = _____ _____
8. can + not = _____ _____
9. you + will = _____ _____
10. he + will = _____ _____

Part II: Rewrite the sentences below, changing the underlined words into contractions. Don't forget to add apostrophes!

1. <u>They will</u> have a party tonight. _____
2. They <u>should not</u> look directly at the sun. _____
3. We <u>can not</u> find our car keys. _____
4. <u>She is</u> waiting for a taxi. _____
5. <u>I am</u> so tired from staying up too late last night. _____

Possessives are words that show ownership. The apostrophe is placed before the final *s*.

Example: Steve's trumpet (*The trumpet belongs to Steve.*)

Part III: Rewrite the following phrases to make possessives. Don't forget the apostrophe!

1. a canary belonging to Mom _____
2. a birthday belonging to John _____
3. a flag belonging to the school _____
4. stripes belonging to the cat _____
5. books belonging to Mr. Frankenstein _____

Part IV: Study the sentences below. Add apostrophes to possessives as needed.

1. Cindy borrowed Mothers photo album.
2. She wanted to study her relatives faces.
3. Grandmas pictures always showed her smiling.
4. Uncle Montys face looked grim.
5. The photo albums pages were falling apart.

Apostrophes in Contractions and Possessives *(cont.)*

Study the pairs of words below. Label one a contraction and the other a possessive. Then use both words in a sentence. The first one has been done for you.

1. wouldn't _____ contraction _____ aardvark's __ possessive __
   __ I wouldn't mess with an aardvark's teeth. __

2. Allison's _____ didn't _____
   _____

3. mustn't _____ rattlesnake's _____
   _____

4. classroom's _____ I'd _____
   _____

5. you're _____ bicycle's _____
   _____

6. shopping mall's _____ shouldn't _____
   _____

7. we're _____ Nancy's _____
   _____

8. I've _____ Mr. Goodall's _____
   _____

9. plant's _____ they're _____
   _____

10. she'll _____ school's _____
    _____

11. Corey's _____ he'll _____
    _____

12. they've _____ amusement park's _____
    _____

13. they'd _____ town's _____
    _____

14. he'd _____ Dr. Sherman's _____
    _____

15. cat's _____ it's _____
    _____

Quotation Marks

Quotation marks should be used any time someone speaks. One set of quotation marks should be placed at the beginning of the quote and one set at the end.

Examples: "Where did you come from?" she asked the ghost.

Peter made a cake, then shouted, "Happy Birthday!" to his father.

Study the sentences below. Add quotation marks where needed.

1. Are you going to take the trash out? Mom asked David.

2. David yawned. "I'm busy playing video games, he said.

3. It won't take itself out, Mom reminded him.

4. I'll do it!" David exclaimed.

5. He'll forget until tonight, Mom muttered to the dog.

6. Woof! said the dog, sniffing the trash can.

7. "David! yelled Mom. "Take out this trash now!

8. Okay, okay," said David. I'm turning off the game.

9. He took out the trash. It stinks, he said.

10. "I'm finished, he told Mother. "Can I have my allowance?

Now, write down a conversation between Jason and Maribelle, who are discussing the big skateboarding competition scheduled for this Saturday. Use at least 10 sentences. Don't forget the quotation marks.

_____

_____

_____

_____

_____

_____

_____

Quotation Marks *(cont.)*

Quotation marks are also used around the titles of poems, songs, and book chapters.

Examples: The teacher read Elizabeth Bishop's poem, "The Fish."

The crowd sang "The Star Spangled Banner" at the ball game.

Look in the chapter titled "Trees" for the information on tree bark.

Study the sentences below. Add quotation marks as needed.

1. Mom and Dad love a poem called The Raven.

2. It's written by a poet named Edgar Allen Poe, who also wrote a poem called Annabelle Lee.

3. Some poems, like Longfellow's The Arrow and the Song, have been turned into choir music.

4. I prefer songs like Take Me Out to the Ball Game.

5. I learned to play Row, Row, Row Your Boat on the trumpet.

6. Next, I'll learn to play Jingle Bells.

7. In Chapter One of my music book, I found all sorts of patriotic songs.

8. Did you know The Star Spangled Banner was first a poem?

9. I want to learn to play You're a Grand Old Flag on my trumpet.

10. Maybe someday I'll write a poem called Ode to My Trumpet and read it to my parents.

Interview your family members. Then fill in the lines below. Don't forget to add quotation marks.

Me: My favorite song is called _____. At school, I learned to sing a song called _____. One teacher taught me a poem titled _____. The poem I like best is called _____.

Family Member #1: A poem _____ remembers from when (he/she) was a child is titled _____. Now, (his/her) favorite poem is _____. (He/She) likes a song called _____. In school, (he/she) sang a song called _____.

Family Member #2: When _____ was a baby, (he/she) sang _____. If (he/she) were going to sing any song in the shower, it would be _____. (His/Her) favorite poem as a child was _____. These days, (He/She) likes a poem called _____.

32

Colons

The **colon** is used between hours and minutes when you are writing out the time.

> Examples: At 2:30 A.M., you'll be able to see the meteor shower.
>
> They were married at exactly 1:30 P.M.

A **colon** is also used in business letter salutations and in written speeches.

> Examples: To Whom It May Concern: My watch broke after one day.
>
> Ladies and Gentlemen: Thank you for your attention.

Study the sentences below. Add colons as needed.

1. The president of the flower society was scheduled to speak at 1145 A.M.

2. Because of a problem with the microphone, she didn't begin her speech until 1215 P.M.

3. She read a speech beginning "Ladies and Gentlemen".

4. "Thank you for agreeing to help us sell flowers at 500 P.M. tomorrow," she read.

5. We should be finished by 800 P.M. so that you can go home for a late dinner.

6. Someone handed the president a note at 1230 P.M.

7. To Whom It May Concern" it said. "Help!"

8. "At exactly 700 P.M. yesterday, a deer ate my roses."

9. "Would someone be willing to donate two plants to me by 700 tomorrow night?"

10. "If the writer of this letter wants to volunteer at our sale tomorrow night, she can have two rose plants by 500 P.M." said the president.

Now, write a short letter to your principal, 5–10 sentences long, in which you suggest the best times for giving students recesses and lunch. Don't forget to use colons!

(date) → _____

_____ ← *(salutation)*

_____

_____

_____

_____

_____

_____

(closing) → _____

(your name) → _____

Semicolons

A **semicolon** links two short related sentences to make a longer sentence. Both of these sentences must have a subject and a predicate before you can link them with a semicolon. Use semicolons to add variety to your writing.

Examples: I like to cook; yesterday, I made dinner for my family.

Swifts are fascinating birds; they nest in chimneys and catch bugs in midair.

We're driving to the snow; we'd better make sure we have chains on our car.

Part I: Study the pairs of sentences below. If they are related, rewrite them as one long sentence, using a semicolon. If they are not related, leave them as is and write "not related."

1. Frida Kahlo is a famous artist. She lived in Mexico and painted pictures.

   _____

2. I'm Kellie's best friend. She always invites me to her birthday parties.

   _____

3. Nisha has always wanted to see Australia. Aphids are taking over Mom's roses.

   _____

4. Pablo cannot stop coughing. His father has gone to buy cough syrup.

   _____

5. Some people say to apply butter to a burned area on the body. This is actually not a good idea.

   _____

6. I need to get glasses. That candle set fire to the curtain.

   _____

7. When handling the American flag, never let it touch the ground. This shows respect for the flag.

   _____

8. Down's Syndrome is a type of developmental disability. Broccoli is not my favorite vegetable.

   _____

9. *The Lion King* is Barbara's favorite play. She's seen it 12 times.

   _____

10. Someday, Susan hopes to ride in a hot air balloon. She'd like to see her house from up in the air.

    _____

Part II: Study the following run-on sentences. Rewrite them correctly, using a semicolon to fix them.

1. Richard Bach wrote about seagulls, later he wrote about airplanes.

2. *Metamorphosis* is a book by Franz Kafka it's about a man who turns into a bug.

3. Chickens make wonderful pets, they'll even come when you call them.

4. Driving on Route 66 is exciting you never know what you'll see.

5. The wedding was cancelled the bride and groom were ill with the flu.

6. They put their house up for sale, they're moving to Alaska.

Hyphens and Dashes

- A **hyphen** is one click on the keyboard. It looks like this: -. Use a hyphen to show a break in words at the end of a sentence.

    Example: She opened the book, and was shocked to see that her grandfather had torn out twenty pages.

You can also use a hyphen in compound nouns.

    Example: My great-aunt worked for Paramount Studios for fifty years.

Finally, use a hyphen in fractions and in numbers from twenty-one to ninety-nine.

    Example: He gave one-half of the forty-two apples to his brother.

- A **dash** is two clicks on the keyboard. It looks like this: — . Use a dash to show emphasis.

    Examples: Most students—not you, of course—do not come to school prepared.
    The bear—a big, black, toothy creature—lumbered toward him.

Study the sentences below. Rewrite them, adding a dash or a hyphen, as indicated by the suggestion at the end of each sentence.

1. My great grandmother broke her hip after falling off a horse. (*hyphen*)

2. The dog a black, skittish Shepherd is almost wild. (*dash*)

3. Earl Hawley a retired actor walks 20 miles a day. (*dash*)

4. It's important to understand the street signs when driv ing a car; otherwise, you could get in an accident. (*hyphen*)

5. I earned seventy two dollars washing dishes after the party. (*hyphen*)

6. Most days but never on Tuesdays they meet for coffee at the local restaurant. (*dash*)

7. He's always lugging around a tuba, which weighs fifty two pounds. (*hyphen*)

8. Dad's mother in law complains about his cooking. (*hyphen*)

9. Learning to read, learning to write, learning to count that's all part of first grade. (*dash*)

10. Until you finish your chores, you cannot play basketball with your friends outside. (*hyphen*)

11. Her heritage she's Scottish is a source of great pride. (*dash*)

12. I need to make one third of this waffle recipe because some people didn't wake up in time for breakfast. (*hyphen*)

13. Ticks are nasty creatures although not as nasty as rattlesnakes which must be removed from your skin immediately. (*dash*)

14. Emily Dickinson wrote hundreds of poems that went unpublished until after her death. (*hyphen*)

15. If you cut this piece of lumber by one fifth, it will make excellent firewood. (*hyphen*)

Putting It All Together III

Study the following sentences and rewrite them on the lines below. Correct punctuation as needed.

1. She cant wait until the choir sings America the Beautiful.

   _____

2. My great grandmother wrote a letter that began, "To Whom It May Concern My motorcycle is broken."

   _____

3. Most dog owners but not me, of course forget to carry plastic bags.

   _____

4. Joe is a superb gardener his tomatoes are bigger than anyone else's!

   _____

5. Come and get it! the cook shouted to the hungry crowd.

   _____

6. Oregons rainfall has been low since March 3 2002.

   _____

7. Read said the teacher, pointing to the poem titled "Ode to a Grecian Urn".

   _____

8. My mother in law will arrive on the 456 P.M. train.

   _____

9. Can't you see that When the Saints Go Marching In is a beautiful song?

   _____

10. The women especially Joyce are working hard to collect food for the poor people of Buffalo New York.

    _____

11. Terris nike tennis shoes are giving her blisters.

    _____

12. Its fun to try new things just yesterday, I learned to polka.

    _____

13. You wont believe what I saw just now mary shouted to her brother.

    _____

14. We have big plans for the summer Mikes aunt is going to teach us to sail.

    _____

15. People mustnt complain if the 345 flight is cancelled.

    _____

Short Story

Using everything that you have learned about grammar and punctuation, write a one-page short story about your life in the space below. Then, ask an adult to read over your work and mark any errors.

_____

_____

_____

_____

_____

_____

_____

_____

_____

_____

_____

_____

_____

_____

_____

_____

_____

_____

_____

_____

Short Story *(cont.)*

Write the final version of your short story below, making sure to correct all errors. You may want to cut out this page and post it in a place for your whole family to read!

38

Assessment

Fill in the bubble in front of the correct answer for each group of possible answers.

1. Aeolus is a Greek god. he is the god of wind.
   - (A) Aeolus is a Greek god; he is the god of wind.
   - (B) Aeolus is a Greek god, he is the god of wind.
   - (C) Aeolus is a Greek god? he is the god of wind.
   - (D) Correct as is

2. Have you read the chapter titled The Industrial revolution?
   - (A) Have you read the chapter titled the industrial revolution?
   - (B) Have you read the chapter titled The Industrial Revolution?
   - (C) Have you read the chapter titled "The Industrial Revolution?"
   - (D) Correct as is

3. They say the Pacific Ocean is warmer than the Atlantic.
   - (A) She say the Pacific Ocean is warmer than the Atlantic.
   - (B) They're say the Pacific Ocean is warmer than the Atlantic.
   - (C) They've say the Pacific Ocean is warmer than the Atlantic.
   - (D) Correct as is

4. Couldnt you study for the test tomorrow?
   - (A) Couldn't you study for the test tomorrow?
   - (B) Could'nt you study for the test tomorrow?
   - (C) Couldn't you study for the test tomorrow!
   - (D) Correct as is

5. She bought a hamster, she bought a duck.
   - (A) She bought a hamster, so she bought a duck.
   - (B) She bought a hamster, nor she bought a duck.
   - (C) She bought a hamster, and she bought a duck.
   - (D) Correct as is

6. I have a twin, and today is their birthday.
   - (A) I have a twin, and today is its birthday.
   - (B) I have a twin, and today is our birthday.
   - (C) I have a twin, and today is we birthday.
   - (D) Correct as is

7. The mosquito carried a disease, it bit the crow.
   - (A) The mosquito carried a disease, and it bit the crow.
   - (B) The mosquito carried a disease it bit the crow.
   - (C) The mosquito carried a disease and it bit the crow.
   - (D) Correct as is

Assessment (cont.)

8. Our teacher grew up in St. Louis, Missouri.

   (A) Our teacher grew up in st. louis, Missouri.

   (B) Our teacher grew up in St. louis, missouri.

   (C) Our teacher grew up in St. Louis Missouri.

   (D) Correct as is

9. She walked slow to the bus stop.

   (A) She walked slowing to the bus stop.

   (B) She walked slowingly to the bus stop.

   (C) She walked slowly to the bus stop.

   (D) Correct as is

10. Dear Mr. Sellers You're my favorite actor.

   (A) Dear Mr. Sellers. You're my favorite actor.

   (B) Dear Mr. Sellers, You're my favorite actor.

   (C) Dear Mr. Sellers! You're my favorite actor.

   (D) Correct as is

11. My brother in law builds model cars in his free time.

   (A) My brother-in-law builds model cars in his free time.

   (B) My brother—in law builds model cars in his free time.

   (C) My brother, in law builds model cars in his free time.

   (D) Correct as is

12. "Watch out for that giant lizard," she shouted.

   (A) "Watch out for that giant lizard?" she shouted.

   (B) "Watch out for that giant lizard." She shouted.

   (C) "Watch out for that giant lizard!" she shouted.

   (D) Correct as is

13. Drape that tablecloth at the table.

   (A) Drape that tablecloth above the table.

   (B) Drape that tablecloth over the table.

   (C) Drape that tablecloth inside the table.

   (D) Correct as is

14. The boy with the purple hair loves classical music.

   (A) The boy with the purple hair

   (B) The boy with the purple hair and a big nose

   (C) Loves classical music by Bach.

   (D) Correct as is

Assessment *(cont.)*

15 Emily belongs to the baptist church in bend, Oregon.

    (A) Emily belongs to the Baptist church in bend, oregon.

    (B) Emily belongs to the Baptist church in Bend, Oregon.

    (C) Emily belongs to the Baptist church in Bend Oregon.

    (D) Correct as is

16. We was so excited about seeing Disneyland!

    (A) We is so excited about seeing Disneyland!

    (B) We's so excited about seeing Disneyland!

    (C) We are so excited about seeing Disneyland!

    (D) Correct as is

17. Bring that students notebook to me.

    (A) Bring that student's notebook to me.

    (B) Bring that students notebooks to me.

    (C) Bring that students's notebooks to me.

    (D) Correct as is

18. She has a ring made of copper, his is made of silver.

    (A) She has a ring made of copper his is made of silver.

    (B) She has a ring made of copper; his is made of silver.

    (C) She has a ring made of copper-his is made of silver.

    (D) Correct as is

19. Cut this recipe down to one-half for the party.

    (A) Cut this recipe down to one—half for the party.

    (B) Cut this recipe down to one, half for the party.

    (C) Cut this recipe down to one half for the party.

    (D) Correct as is

20. Have you ever read Frost's poem "Stopping by Woods on a Snowy Evening?

    (A) Have you ever read Frost's poem "Stopping by Woods on a Snowy Evening?"

    (B) Have you ever read Frost's poem Stopping by Woods on a Snowy Evening?

    (C) Have you ever read "Frost's" poem Stopping by Woods on a Snowy Evening?

    (D) Correct as is

21. Climb above that fence and untie the cow.

    (A) Climb inside that fence and untie the cow.

    (B) Climb into the fence and untie the cow.

    (C) Climb over the fence and untie the cow.

    (D) Correct as is

Assessment (cont.)

22. Did you see the flock of geeses flying overhead?
    - (A) Did you see the flock of geese's flying overhead?
    - (B) Did you see the flock of geese flying overhead?
    - (C) Did you see the flock of gooses flying overhead?
    - (D) Correct as is

23. She studied, yet she earned a "D" on her test.
    - (A) She studied, so she earned a "D" on her test.
    - (B) She studied yet she earned a "D" on her test.
    - (C) She studied, for she earned a "D" on her test.
    - (D) Correct as is

24. "You're driving me crazy," shouted Paul.
    - (A) "You're driving me crazy!" shouted Paul.
    - (B) "You're driving me crazy?" shouted Paul.
    - (C) "You're driving me crazy." Shouted Paul.
    - (D) Correct as is

25. Has two earrings in her ear.
    - (A) Has two silver earrings in her ear.
    - (B) Margaret has two silver earrings in her ear.
    - (C) Has two silver earrings in her ear lobe.
    - (D) Correct as is

26. Steve and Steve's friends play at Steve's house.
    - (A) Steve and Steve's friends play at his house.
    - (B) Steve and Steve's friends play at her house.
    - (C) Steve and his friends play at his house.
    - (D) Correct as is

27. To Whom It May Concern: My new dishwasher is broken.
    - (A) To Whom It May Concern. My new dishwasher is broken.
    - (B) To Whom It May Concern, my new dishwasher is broken.
    - (C) To Whom It may Concern? My new dishwasher is broken.
    - (D) Correct as is

28. Many kids—not you, of course don't like homework.
    - (A) Many kids—not you, of course—don't like homework.
    - (B) Many kids-not you, of course-don't like homework.
    - (C) Many kids, not you, of course, don't like homework.
    - (D) Correct as is

Assessment (cont.)

29. Mario is Ecuadorian; he's lived in the US a year.

    (A) Mario is ecuadorian; he's lived in the U.S. a year.

    (B) Mario is Ecuadorian; he's lived in the U.S. a year.

    (C) Mario is Ecuadorian, he's lived in the U.S. a year.

    (D) Correct as is

30. Mary was the guest of honor it was her birthday.

    (A) Mary was the guest of honor, it was her birthday.

    (B) Mary was the guest of honor. it was her birthday.

    (C) Mary was the guest of honor, for it was her birthday.

    (D) Correct as is

31. Can you see the film over that mans' head?

    (A) Can you see the film over that men's head?

    (B) Can you see the film over that man's head?

    (C) Can you see the film over that mens' head?

    (D) Correct as is

32. Jacques is a tall man.

    (A) Jacques is a tallest man.

    (B) Jacques is a talling man.

    (C) Jacques is a less tall man.

    (D) Correct as is

33. Dr farnsworth checked the patient for symptoms.

    (A) Dr Farnsworth checked the patient for symptoms.

    (B) Dr. farnsworth checked the patient for symptoms.

    (C) Dr. Farnsworth checked the patient for symptoms.

    (D) Correct as is

34. The train leaves at 54:5 P.M.

    (A) The train leaves at 545 P.M.

    (B) The train leaves at 5:45 P.M.

    (C) The train leaves at 545: P.M.

    (D) Correct as is

35. James learned to drive tomorrow.

    (A) James will learn to drive tomorrow.

    (B) James learning to drive tomorrow.

    (C) James have learned to drive tomorrow.

    (D) Correct as is

36. Waltzing Matilda is my favorite song.

    Ⓐ "waltzing matilda" is my favorite song.

    Ⓑ "waltzing Matilda" is my favorite song.

    Ⓒ "Waltzing Matilda" is my favorite song.

    Ⓓ Correct as is

37. The dogs' new collar fit him perfectly.

    Ⓐ The dog's new collar fit him perfectly.

    Ⓑ The dogs's new collar fit him perfectly.

    Ⓒ The dogs new collar fit him perfectly.

    Ⓓ Correct as is

38. Joan loves to act, she's got the lead in the school play.

    Ⓐ Joan loves to act; she's got the lead in the school play.

    Ⓑ Joan loves to act; but she's got the lead in the school play.

    Ⓒ Joan loves to act she's got the lead in the school play.

    Ⓓ Correct as is

39. Those students never line up properly.

    Ⓐ Those students never lines up properly.

    Ⓑ Those students never lining up properly.

    Ⓒ Those students never has lines up properly.

    Ⓓ Correct as is

40. Thank you for the flowers. Sincerely Judy

    Ⓐ Thank you for the flowers. Sincerely, Judy

    Ⓑ Thank you for the flowers, sincerely, judy

    Ⓒ Thank you for the flowers, sincerely. Judy

    Ⓓ Correct as is

41. They found the japanese art to be fascinating.

    Ⓐ they found the Japanese Art to be fascinating.

    Ⓑ They found the japanese Art to be fascinating

    Ⓒ They found the Japanese art to be fascinating.

    Ⓓ Correct as is

42. Would'nt you be more comfortable in this chair?

    Ⓐ Wouldnt you be more comfortable in this chair?

    Ⓑ Wouldn't you be more comfortable in this chair?

    Ⓒ Wouldn't' you be more comfortable in this chair?

    Ⓓ Correct as is

Answer Key

Page 4

1. (Great-horned owls) are at the top of the food chain.
2. (They) can survive almost anywhere.
3. (These owls) eat rodents, insects, and even skunks.
4. (Outdoor cats) are not safe from these winged predators.
5. (The ears on Great-horned owls) are lopsided.
6. (This) allows them to pinpoint the exact location of their prey.
7. (A Great-horned owl's eyes) work like binoculars.
8. (No small animal, bird, or insect) can hide from these owls.
9. (The flight feathers on a Great-horned owl) are serrated.
10. (These feathers allow the owl) to fly silently through the forest.
11. (Cliffs and trees) make excellent nesting sites for owls.
12. (Other birds' nests) are fair game, too.
13. (Great-horned owls) are amazing creatures.
14. (You) can see them at dusk.
15. (Their call) is distinctive and haunting.

Page 5

Part I
Answers will vary.

Part II
1. family
2. sister-in-law
3. trolley car
4. herd
5. class
6. editor-in-chief
7. pile
8. passers-by
9. flock
10. group

Page 6

1. Paul's
2. city's
3. boys'
4. day's
5. women's
6. boy's
7. no corrections
8. bike's
9. month's
10. thorn's
11. father's
12. no corrections
13. geese's
14. heart's
15. girl's

Page 7

Part I
1. babies
2. matches
3. foxes
4. turkeys
5. parties
6. dresses
7. lilies
8. cries
9. wishes
10. cities

Part II
1. beliefs
2. geese
3. sisters-in-law
4. wolves
5. men
6. sheep
7. passersby
8. feet
9. deer
10. chiefs

Page 8

Connie looked forward to Sixth Grade Nature Camp with all <u>her</u> heart. Her friends Joanne, Debi, and Lyddie could hardly wait, either. On the morning <u>they</u> were to go to camp, <u>they</u> put <u>their</u> suitcases in the bus. Connie sat down next to <u>her</u> best friend. The driver started the bus and guided it out onto the road. The bus climbed high into the mountains. They were beautiful, with trees thickly covering <u>them</u>. Connie and <u>her</u> friend stared out the window in delight. "<u>I'm</u> so happy she finally gets to go to camp!" Connie told <u>her</u> friend. The boy behind her took a picture of <u>her</u> with <u>his</u> camera. "Smile!" <u>he</u> said to Connie, and Connie smiled <u>her</u> best smile. The driver pulled the bus into a parking lot, and <u>she</u> helped the kids get their bags off the bus. It was time to camp!

Page 9

Part I
1. his or her
2. her
3. our
4. his or her
5. their
6. his
7. their
8. his or her
9. his
10. their

Page 10

Part I
1. helping
2. helping
3. action
4. helping
5. action
6. linking
7. helping
8. action
9. linking
10. helping

Page 11

Part I
1. flew
2. swam
3. cried
4. drank
5. went
6. sped
7. ran
8. sang
9. drew
10. ate
11. bought
12. spoke
13. rode
14. wore
15. grew
16. froze
17. made
18. slept
19. bit
20. sent

Part II
1. went
2. am
3. threw
4. groans
5. ran
6. hid
7. are going
8. broke
9. will live
10. earned

Page 12

Seven students <u>are</u> planning a trip to the snow. We <u>are</u> going to ski, snowshoe, and sled until we <u>are</u> so tired that we <u>fall</u> into bed at night. My mom will go, and she <u>is</u> really excited about making hot chocolate for all of us. She just <u>bought</u> new skis for the occasion. I <u>need</u> new long underwear, and I could use a hat and some mittens. My friend Joe <u>wants</u> a snowboard; his mom <u>is</u> going to buy him one for his birthday. My friends and I <u>are</u> looking for cabins to rent. We <u>are</u> having a car wash to raise money. I <u>hope</u> to get good at skiing so I can <u>join</u> my friends on the intermediate slopes. Winter sports <u>are</u> a lot of fun, as long as you <u>have</u> the right equipment and warm clothes.

Answer Key (cont.)

Page 13

1. subject
2. subject
3. subject
4. subject
5. verb
6. verb
7. verb
8. subject
9. subject
10. verb

Pages 14–15

Answers will vary

Pages 16–17

Answers will vary.

Page 18

Part I

1. in
2. on
3. beneath
4. on
5. around
6. during
7. across
8. between
9. for
10. for
11. inside, for
12. outside

Part II

Answers will vary

Page 20

Answers will vary.

Page 21

Part I

1. (He) didn't bring the soup, [nor] did (he) remember the bread.
2. (I) trained for months, [yet] (I) couldn't finish the race.
3. Would (you) like to ski, [or] would (you) prefer to snowboard?
4. (I) don't know Spanish, [but] (I) do know some French.
5. (She) saw the movie three times, [for] (she) really loved the leading actress.
6. (The postal worker) is here, [so] (I) have to answer the door.
7. (They) raise Angora cats, [and] (they) also have three dogs.

Part II

Answers will vary

Page 22

Answers will vary.

Page 23

Answers will vary.

Page 24

1. My friend Mike loves to collect old books.
2. Every Friday, he goes to Mr. Beedle's bookstore to look for books.
3. Sometimes, Mr. Beedle leaves a note for Mike on Thursday.
4. "Dear Mike," it says, "I have a new book for you."
5. "Don't forget to bring your money. Sincerely, Mr. Beedle."
6. The bookstore is located at 323 Charnelton Lane in Philadelphia.
7. Mike takes the bus and gets off on Franklin Street.
8. He walks into the bookstore and says, "Hello!"
9. "Greetings!" says Mr. Beedle. "Welcome!"
10. On New Year's Day, Mike invites Mr. Beedle to his house.
11. "Bring your mom!" Mike says.
12. "Can I bring Dad, too?" Mr. Beedle asks Mike.
13. "Does he like books?" Mike asks.
14. The family shows up at 55 Clark Street on December 31st.
15. "We brought you socks! Mr. Beedle's father says to mike.

Page 25

1. Cabrillo Elementary School
2. Catholic
3. cucumbers
4. *Los Angeles Times*
5. Unicycle
6. "Frosty the Snowman"
7. *Charlotte's Web*
8. Coca Cola
9. kitten
10. English class
11. Sony
12. Italian
13. pine tree
14. the Mona Lisa
15. University of Southern California
16. Toys R Us

Page 26

Part I

1. JoJo found a suitcase bearing the initials L.S.
2. The suitcase sat at the intersection between Main St. and Third Ave., under a tree.
3. "Is this yours?" she asked Dr. Smith.
4. "No," he said. "Try the Rev. Sanders at the Baptist Church."
5. "Is that the church on Blanket St.?" asked JoJo.
6. "Yes. Ms. Rimbaud should be there now," Dr. Smith said.
7. JoJo made a quick stop at her P.O. box for her mail.
8. Then she took the suitcase to Ms. Rimbaud in the church office.
9. "There was no i.d. on this suitcase," she said.
10. Rev. Sanders is out buying groceries, paper plates, etc. for the church picnic," Ms. Rimbaud said.
11. "Leave the suitcase here, and Mr. Roberts, the janitor, will give it to him."
12. JoJo drove down Sullivan Rd. toward her house.
13. She saw many cars with U.S. flags on their windows.
14. On Lansing Blvd., she pulled into a driveway.
15. There on her doorstep, sat another suitcase bearing the initials J.J.

Part II

1. Ave.
2. St.
3. Rd.
4. Pl.
5. Mr.
6. Mrs.
7. Dr.
8. etc.
9. i.d.
10. P.O.
11. Rev.
12. Blvd.
13. U.S.
14. U.P.S.

Answer Key *(cont.)*

Page 27

1. Ms. King teaches sixth graders in Oxnard, California.
2. She'll take them to Europe on June 20, 2003.
3. First, they'll go to London, England.
4. After they see Buckingham Palace, they'll go to Paris, France.
5. On July 4th, 2003, they'll go to Greece.
6. Athens, Greece, is the home of the Acropolis.
7. The students will see the birthplace of the Olympics in Olympia, Greece.
8. Finally, they'll head for home on July 6th, 2003.
9. Their plane stops for an hour in Frankfurt, Germany.
10. It lands a day later in Los Angeles, California.
11. "Dear Mrs. King," the students wrote.
12. "Thank you for taking us to Europe. Love, your students.
13. Mrs. King replied from her home in Oak View, California.
14. "Dear students," she typed on her computer.
15. "I had a wonderful time. Did you? Sincerely, Mrs. King."

Page 28

1. Mrs. Mandy Murphy checked her P.O. box this afternoon.
2. There was a invitation from Dr. Frank Simpson.
3. "Dear Julie," the letter read.
4. "Please come to a surprise party for Mrs. Cathy Simpson."
5. "There will be food, beverages, etc., plus a live band."
6. "I hope you can make it. Sincerely, Frank."
7. Mrs. Murphy looked at the initials on the bottom of the letter, which read "F.S."
8. "Who are the Simpsons?" she wondered.
9. A woman beside her opened her P.O. box. "Where is my party invitation?" she exclaimed.
10. Mrs. Murphy held out Dr. Simpson's invitation.
11. "Is this yours?" she asked.
12. Ms. Julie Sheridan looked at the invitation.
13. "Yes!" she cried. "I thought I wasn't invited."
14. "Thank you," she told Mrs. Murphy. "Would you like to come to a surprise party?"

Page 29

Part I

1. I'll; wi
2. shouldn't; o
3. we're; a
4. she's; i
5. they're; a
6. I'm; a
7. couldn't; o
8. can't; no
9. you'll; wi
10. he'll; wi

Part II

1. They'll
2. shouldn't
3. can't
4. she's
5. I'm

Part III

1. Mom's canary
2. John's birthday
3. school's flag
4. cat's stripes
5. Mr. Frankenstein's books

Part IV

1. Cindy borrowed Mother's photo album.
2. She wanted to study her relative's faces.
3. Grandma's pictures always showed her smiling.
4. Uncle Monty's face looked grim.
5. The photo album's pages were falling apart.

Page 30

1. contraction, possessive
2. possessive, contraction
3. contraction, possessive
4. possessive, contraction
5. contraction, possessive
6. possessive, contraction
7. contraction, possessive
8. contraction, possessive
9. possessive, contraction
10. contraction, possessive
11. possessive, contraction
12. contraction, possessive
13. contraction, possessive
14. contraction, possessive
15. possessive, contraction

Page 31

1. "Are you going to take the trash out?" Mom asked David.
2. David yawned. "I'm busy playing video games," he said.
3. "It won't take itself out," Mom reminded him.
4. "I'll do it!" David exclaimed.
5. "He'll forget until tonight," Mom muttered to the dog.
6. "Woof!" said the dog, sniffing the trash can.
7. "David!" yelled Mom. "Take out this trash now!"
8. "Okay, okay," said David. "I'm turning off the game."
9. He took out the trash. "It stinks," he said.
10. "I'm finished," he told Mother. "Can I have my allowance?"

Page 32

1. Mom and Dad love a poem called "The Raven."
2. It's written by a poet named Edgar Allen Poe, who also wrote a poem called "Annabelle Lee."
3. Some poems, like Longfellow's "The Arrow and the Song," have been turned into choir music.
4. I prefer songs like "Take Me Out to the Ball Game."
5. I learned to play "Row, Row, Row Your Boat" on the trumpet.
6. Next, I'll learn to play "Jingle Bells."
7. In "Chapter One" of my music book, I found all sorts of patriotic songs.
8. Did you know "The Star Spangled Banner" was first a poem?
9. I want to learn to play "You're a Grand Old Flag" on my trumpet.
10. Maybe someday I'll write a poem called "Ode to My Trumpet" and read it to my parents.

Page 33

1. The president of the flower society was scheduled to speak at 11:45 A.M.
2. Because of a problem with the microphone, she didn't begin her speech until 12:15 P.M.
3. She read a speech beginning "Ladies and Gentlemen:".
4. "Thank you for agreeing to help us sell flowers at 5:00 P.M. tomorrow," she read.
5. We should be finished by 8:00 P.M. so that you can go home for a late dinner.
6. Someone handed the president a note at 12:30 P.M.
7. To Whom It May Concern:" it said. "Help!"
8. "At exactly 7:00 P.M. yesterday, a deer ate my roses."
9. "Would someone be willing to donate two plants to me by 7:00 tomorrow night?"
10. "If the writer of this letter wants to volunteer at our sale tomorrow night, she can have two rose plants by 5:00 P.M." said the president.

Answer Key *(cont.)*

Page 34

Part I

1. Frida Kahlo is a famous artist; she lived in Mexico and painted pictures.
2. I'm Kellie's best friend; she always invites me to her birthday parties.
3. not related
4. Pablo cannot stop coughing; his father has gone to buy cough syrup.
5. Some people say to apply butter to a burned area on the body; this is actually not a good idea.
6. not related
7. When handling the American flag, never let it touch the ground; this shows respect for the flag.
8. not related
9. *The Lion King* is Barbara's favorite play; she's seen it 12 times.
10. Someday, Susan hopes to ride in a hot air balloon; she'd like to see her house from up in the air.

Part II

1. Richard Bach wrote about seagulls; later he wrote about airplanes.
2. *Metamorphosis* is a book by Franz Kafka; it's about a man who turns into a bug.
3. Chickens make wonderful pets; they'll even come when you call them.
4. Driving on Route 66 is exciting; you never know what you'll see.
5. The wedding was cancelled; the bride and groom were ill with the flu.
6. They put their house up for sale; they're moving to Alaska.

Page 35

1. My great-grandmother broke her hip after falling off a horse.
2. The dog—a black, skittish Shepherd—is almost wild.
3. Earl Hawley—a retired actor—walks 20 miles a day.
4. It's important to understand the street signs when driv-ing a car; otherwise, you could get in an accident.
5. I earned seventy-two dollars washing dishes after the party.
6. Most days—but never on Tuesdays—they meet for coffee at the local restaurant.
7. He's always lugging around a tuba, which weighs fifty-two pounds.
8. Dad's mother-in-law complains about his cooking.
9. Learning to read, learning to write, and learning to count—that's all part of first grade.
10. Until you finish your chores, you cannot play basket-ball with your friends outside.
11. Her heritage—she's Scottish—is a source of great pride.
12. I need to make one-third of this waffle recipe because some people didn't wake up in time for breakfast.
13. Ticks are nasty creatures—although not as nasty as rattlesnakes—which must be removed from your skin immediately.
14. Emily Dickinson wrote hundreds of poems, which went unpub-lished until after her death.
15. If you cut this piece of lumber by one-fifth, it will make excellent firewood.

Page 36

1. She can't wait until the choir sings "America the Beautiful."
2. My great-grandmother wrote a letter that began, "To Whom It May Concern: My motorcycle is broken."
3. Most dog owners—but not me, of course—forget to carry plastic bags.
4. Joe is a superb gardener; his tomatoes are bigger than anyone else's!
5. "Come and get it!" the cook shouted to the hungry crowd.
6. Oregon's rainfall has been low since March 3, 2002.
7. "Read," said the teacher, pointing to the poem titled "Ode to a Grecian Urn".
8. My mother-in-law will arrive on the 4:56 P.M. train.
9. Can't you see that "When the Saints Go Marching In" is a beautiful song?
10. The women—especially Joyce—are working hard to collect food for the poor people of Buffalo, New York.
11. Terri's Nike tennis shoes are giving her blisters.
12. It's fun to try new things; just yesterday, I learned to polka.
13. "You won't believe what I saw just now!" Mary shouted to her brother.
14. We have big plans for the summer; Mike's aunt is going to teach us to sail.
15. People mustn't complain if the 3:45 flight is canceled.

Pages 39–45

1. A	22. B
2. C	23. D
3. D	24. A
4. A	25. B
5. C	26. C
6. B	27. D
7. A	28. A
8. D	29. B
9. C	30. C
10. B	31. B
11. A	32. D
12. C	33. C
13. B	34. B
14. D	35. A
15. B	36. C
16. C	37. A
17. A	38. A
18. B	39. D
19. D	40. A
20. A	41. C
21. C	42. B